The Pepper Pantry:
Jalapeños

Dave DeWitt, the Pope of Peppers

For George — Enjoy the most famous pepper of all! Dave

Terra Nova Books
SANTA FE, NEW MEXICO

Terra Nova Books

The Pepper Pantry: Jalapeños. Copyright © 2013 by Dave DeWitt. All rights reserved. Printed in the United States of America. No part of this book may be used or reproduced in any manner whatsoever without written permission except in the case of brief quotations embodied in critical articles and reviews. Send inquiries to Terra Nova Books, 33 Alondra Road, Santa Fe, New Mexico 87508.

Published by Terra Nova Books, Santa Fe, New Mexico.
www.TerraNovaBooks.com

ISBN 978-1-482597-97-4

Contents

INTRODUCTION

PART 1: THE MOST FAMOUS CHILE PEPPER EVER?
    The Plant 6
    Agriculture 6
    Jalapeño Varieties 7
    Growing Jalapeños 8
    Seeds and Seedlings 8
    The Plot Thickens 9
    Flowering and Fruiting 10
    Harvesting the Heat 11
    Vitamins and the Thermo-Nutrient Principle 11
    Fame 12
    Culinary Usage 13

PART 2: JALAPEÑOS IN THE KITCHEN
    Preserving Jalapeños 16
    Salsas, Sauces, and Dressings 20
    Breakfast 28
    Appetizers, Soups, and Salads 30
    Main Dishes and Vegetarian Sides 44
    Breads 61
    A Drink and a Dessert 64

PART 3: RESOURCES
    Further Reading 68
    Seed and Plant Sources 68
    Websites 68
    Chile Pepper Suppliers and Online Hotshops 69

INTRODUCTION

In 1997, I worked with the team of Nancy Gerlach and Chuck Evans to produce the first two books in the Pepper Pantry series, *The Pepper Pantry: Habanero* and *The Pepper Pantry: Chipotle*. Although both sold well and are still in print, the publisher chose not to continue the series, and the current technology for print-on-demand and ebooks was not in place then. So I'm continuing the Pepper Pantry series now by producing short how-to books at a reasonable price, and the first title is this one, *The Pepper Pantry: Jalapeños.* Finally, one of the most popular peppers in the world gets its due, and I hope readers and cooks enjoy growing and eating these legendary chile peppers.

PART 1

The Most Famous Chile Pepper Ever?

The Plant

The jalapeño pepper was named for the town of Jalapa, Mexico, where it was originally marketed. It was not originally grown there but was imported from the surrounding region. The pods are thick-walled, conical, dark green when immature though most turn red at maturity, and with high heat. The fruit skin may show a brown netting pattern called corkiness. This does not affect the flavor and is desirable in Mexico but not so in the U.S. Because the thick fruit walls keep the pod from drying naturally on the plant, the mature red jalapeños are dried by being smoked over mesquite or another hardwood, and the product is called chipotle.

Jalapeños usually grow from two to three feet tall. They have a compact single stem or an upright, multi-branched, spreading habit. The leaves are light to dark green and measure about three inches long and two inches wide. It takes about seventy to eighty days from sowing to when the green pods are ready for harvest. Each plant produces about twenty-five to thirty-five pods, generally green (occasionally, sunlight will cause purpling), maturing to red.

Agriculture

In Mexico, approximately forty thousand acres are cultivated commercially in three main agricultural zones: the Lower Palaloapan River Valley in the states of Veracruz and Oaxaca, northern Veracruz, and the area around Delicias, Chihuahua. This latter region grows the jalapeños that are processed and exported to the U.S. Approximately 60 percent of the Mexican jalapeño crop is used for processing, 20 percent for fresh consumption, and 20 percent to produce chipotle chiles, smoked jalapeños.

In the United States, approximately fifty-five hundred acres are under cultivation, with Texas the leading state for jalapeño production, followed by New Mexico. Home gardeners should remember that the U.S. varieties of jalapeños flourish better in semi-arid climates—ones with dry air combined with irrigation. If planted in hot and humid zones in the U.S. during the summer, the yield decreases, and so Mexican varieties should be grown.

Jalapeño Varieties

Because the jalapeños have been selected and bred for thousands of years, they have developed unique flavors. Most commercial jalapeños are preserved by canning or pickling, while a small amount are dehydrated in either the green or red stage. Most jalapeños from the home garden are used fresh in salsas, sliced into rings for use with nachos, or pickled for later use. My five favorites are "Early Jalapeño," "NuMex Jalmundo," "NuMex Piñata," "NuMex Primavera," and "NuMex Vaquero."

"Early Jalapeño," as the name implies, matures before other cultivars. It will be ready to pick about a week or two before other jalapeños. The plant will reach twenty-four inches, the height of most jalapeños. "NuMex Jalmundo" has large fruits with little corkiness. Its high yields and sweetness are not found in other jalapeños.

"NuMex Piñata" originated spontaneously in the cultivar "Early Jalapeño." "NuMex Piñata" is unique in the transition of colors that the pods undergo as they mature. Immature fruit are light green, maturing to yellow, orange, and finally red. The foliage of "Early Jalapeño" and other jalapeño cultivars is dark green, while "NuMex Piñata" has golden-yellow foliage. The plant growth habit of "NuMex Piñata" is smaller and tends to decline earlier in the season because of the lack of chlorophyll produced by the foliage. "NuMex Piñata" is a unique jalapeño for making colorful salsa. It has kept the natural flavors and aromas of traditional jalapeños and is considered hot, with a heat level of 50,000 Scoville Heat Units (SHUs). Most characteristics of the plant and fruit, such as height, yield, and pod width, are not significantly different from those of "Early Jalapeño," but the pod is longer.

"NuMex Primavera" has pods with rounded shoulders, little to no corkiness, a semi-pointed tip that is characteristic of the standard jalapeño shape, and a dark green color caused by the absence of anthocyanin which would change it to red as it matures. "NuMex Primavera" displays a uniformly mild heat level of 8,000 SHUs, much milder than industry standard jalapeños. Its fruits are two inches long and one inch wide, and have thick walls. "NuMex Primavera" is a favorite of home gardeners because of its mild heat and the presence of traditional flavors and aromas.

"NuMex Vaquero" is an open-pollinated jalapeño that produces yields at the same level as F1 hybrids. It has tolerance to the root rot disease pathogen *Phytophthora capsici*. The pod is green without purpling and has smooth skin (no corkiness), a blunted tip, rounded shoulders, multiple locules, and uniform heat. Pods are two and a half inches long and almost one inch wide. The heat level of "NuMex Vaquero" is 25,000 to 30,000 SHUs, similar to that of "Early Jalapeño."

Growing Jalapeños

Seeds for jalapeño varieties are available from local nurseries and sources listed in the Resources section at the end of this book. Or you can buy bedding plants from ChilePlants.com and go right to the hardening off phase before planting in the garden or containers.

Seeds and Seedlings

About six weeks before transplanting seedlings into the garden, start the seeds in plastic six-pack seedling growers, just as commercial greenhouses do. Use a vermiculite-based growing medium rather than soil because the seedlings' roots receive more oxygen and thus grow faster.

The six-packs are set in trays on top of heating wire or tape to keep soil temperatures above seventy-five degrees, since the warmth of the soil can radically improve the germination percentage of most chile varieties.

The seedlings should be grown in full sun in a greenhouse or window so they do not become "leggy" and topple over. Some leggy seedlings may be pinched back to make a bushier plant and ensure that leaf growth does not overwhelm stem growth. Keep the seedlings moist but not wet; overwatering will cause stem rot. It will also be necessary to fertilize the plants after they have put out their first true leaves. Use an all-purpose, water-soluble fertilizer (15-30-15), one-quarter teaspoon to a gallon of water, every time the seedlings are watered. When growing seedlings in the house, remember that cats love to graze on tender young plants—which will not harm the cats but will destroy the chiles.

Chile peppers should not be set out in the garden until after the last frost, and ideally should not be set out until the temperature of the garden soil four inches below the surface reaches sixty-five degrees. Before transplanting, the seedlings should be "hardened-off" by placing the trays outside for a few hours each day during warm, sunny days. Constant movement of the seedlings from light breezes will strengthen the stems and prepare the plants for the rigors of the garden. Chile pepper gardeners living in particularly chilly regions should wait until the plants blossom before planting them in the garden.

THE PLOT THICKENS

If the garden plot is to be irrigated, use a shovel to make rows and furrows, and then set the chile pepper plants two feet apart. Though more plants could be crammed into the garden, or the square footage reduced, this size and spacing works best for me mainly because it lets me harvest the pods without stomping on the plants. Some gardeners place the chiles as close as one foot apart so the plants will shade each other and protect the fruit from sunburn. If necessary, protect the young chile plants from freak frosts and cutworms by covering them with glass or plastic jars at night.

After transplanting the chiles, the garden should be thoroughly mulched. Use several layers of newspaper in hot climates or black plastic film in cool summer climates. Where summer temperatures regularly are in the nineties, black plastic in a garden can raise the temperature in that microclimate so high that the plants will stop flowering. Layers of newspaper weighted down with soil reflect sunlight, hold water, and provide additional organic material for the soil after they disintegrate.

Chiles need regular water and plenty of it, but overwatering is the biggest mistake of the home gardener. Well-drained soil is the key here, and the first indication of overwatering is water standing in the garden for any length of time. Some wilting of the plants in the hot summer sun is normal and does not always mean the plants need water.

A high-nitrogen fertilizer encourages foliage growth but should be discontinued after flowering. Some people encourage root growth by adding a teaspoon of phosphate two inches below the planting hole during transplanting.

FLOWERING AND FRUITING

To set fruit, the plants require daytime temperatures between sixty-five and eighty degrees and night temperatures above fifty-five. Flowering decreases during the hottest months of the summer, and, in fact, extremely hot or dry conditions will result in the blossoms' dropping off the plant. However, in the early fall, flowering picks up again, although in northern regions, fall blooms are unlikely to yield fruit. In most locations, the first hard frost will kill the plants, and the remaining pods then should be removed.

I am often asked if cultivation techniques can alter the amount of capsaicin in the pods and make the chiles hotter or milder. The amount of capsaicin in chiles is genetically fixed, which means that the plants will breed true to their heat levels under ideal conditions. However, undue stress on the plants in the form of heat, drought, or flooding can dramatically increase the heat levels, according to researchers at New Mexico State University. There is no known gardening procedure for decreasing the capsaicin in the pods, but the same effect can be achieved in the kitchen by the diluting or buffering techniques I discuss a little later.

Harvesting the Heat

I recommend the technique of staggered harvesting, which means that the chiles in the garden can be used all year long after many of them are preserved, using methods I discuss in Part 2. Usually the first chiles available are the small ones that are used green in fresh salsas—like your favorite jalapeños, for example. It is important to continue harvesting the ripe pods as they mature. If the pods are allowed to remain on the plant, few new ones will form, whereas if the pods are continually harvested, the plants will produce great numbers of pods. The best time to pick chiles for drying is when they first start to turn red. This timing will stimulate the plant into further production, and the harvested chiles can be strung to dry and will turn bright red. When harvesting, it is best to cut the peppers off the plants with a knife or scissors because the branches are brittle and will often break before the stem of the chile pod will.

Vitamins and the Thermo-Nutrient Principle

The heat levels of jalapeños are particularly important because of their reputation for burning out people's gullets. Actually, jalapeños are thermo-nutrients—they are both hot and healthy. Pepper pods are low in calories, cholesterol, and salt but high in fiber and vitamins. A green jalapeño pod contains twice the amount of vitamin C as a Valencia orange, and a mere ounce of them will provide the minimum daily requirement for C. As the green pods turn red, the vitamin A content increases dramatically until the red chile jalapeño contains twice the amount of a carrot.

Despite these impressive vitamin statistics, the health aspects of chile peppers are usually overshadowed by their burning pungency. The heat source of chile peppers is a complex of seven closely related alkaloid compounds called capsaicinoids. These compounds, commonly called capsaicin, are produced by glands at the junction of the placenta and the pod wall. The capsaicin spreads unevenly throughout the inside of the pod but is concentrated mostly in the placental tissue. The seeds are not sources of heat, as is commonly believed. However, because of their proximity to the placenta, the seeds do occasionally absorb capsaicin through processing. Jalapeños measure between 2,500 and 10,000 SHUs, depending on the variety and growing conditions, except for the varieties "NuMex Piñata" and "NuMex Vaquero," which are much hotter. Compare this to New Mexican green chiles, which rarely exceed 1,000 SHUs. Contrary to popular belief, jalapeños do not cause stomach ulcers no matter how hot they are.

Food that is too hot to be eaten comfortably can be cooled down by either diluting or buffering. Diluting is simple—a quart of jalapeño chile stew containing one pepper pod is obviously hotter than a gallon of chile stew with one pod. Buffering involves use of substances that counteract the burning sensation of the capsaicin, especially dairy products such as milk, yogurt, and ice cream—the thicker the better. For capsaicin-burned hands, a soaking in ordinary cooking oil seems to work best.

FAME

Jalapeños are one of the most famous chile peppers. They are instantly recognizable, and a considerable mythology has sprung up about them, particularly in Texas. The impetus for the popularity of jalapeños starts from a combination of their unique taste, their heat, and their continued use as a snack food.

In 1956, *Newsweek* magazine published a story on a pepper-eating contest held in the Bayou Teche country of Louisiana, near the home of the famous Tabasco® sauce. The article rated the jalapeño as "the hottest pepper known," more fiery than the "green tabasco" or "red cayenne." That was the extent of chile pepper "knowledge" in the '50s! Thus the Tex-Mex chile was launched as the perfectly pungent pepper for jalapeño-eating contests, which have proliferated all over the country.

John Espinosa of San Antonio, Texas, gulped his way into the 1988 *Guinness Book of World Records* by consuming an amazing twenty-nine jalapeño chiles in two minutes flat! His record eclipsed by two the number that Joe Marquez of Roswell, New Mexico, had swallowed in September, 1987. In 1992, Braulio Ramirez earned the title of Jalapeño King at the Laredo, Texas, Jalapeño Festival by consuming an astonishing 141 jalapeños in fifteen minutes. He barely beat out Jed Donahue, who consumed more than 150 jalapeños but was disqualified for vomiting. The current record for the most jalapeños eaten during a contest was set in 2011 by professional eater Patrick "Deep Dish" Bertoletti at a very hot (and painful) 275 pickled jalapeños in eight minutes! Considering these astonishing chile pepper consumption records, it's no wonder that a demographics magazine once suggested the southwestern part of Texas be separated into a new state named "Jalapeño."

CULINARY USAGE

Many jalapeños are used straight out of the garden in salsas. Others are pickled in escabeche and sold to restaurants and food services for salad bars. Jalapeños are processed as "nacho slices" and "nacho rings" that are served over nachos, one of the most popular snack foods in arenas and ball parks. Jalapeños are commonly used in commercial salsas and picante sauces, which account for a large percentage of the imports from Mexico. And far north of Texas, Chicagoans are feasting these days on jalapeño bagels with salsa cream cheese at one of the many bagel franchises there. In home cooking, jalapeños are a part of a vast number of different types of fiery foods, from breakfasts to desserts in the cooking of countries as diverse as Costa Rica and China, as the following recipes indicate.

PART 2
Jalapeños in the Kitchen

Preserving Jalapeños

Drying and Powders

Either green or red jalapeños can be dried—outdoors if you live in a low-humidity climate or in a food dehydrator in a moist climate. Simply wash the pods, cut them in half lengthwise, place them on thick black plastic in the sun, and cover them with cheesecloth to keep insects off. Or follow the instructions that came with your food dehydrator for drying fruits and vegetables. The jalapeños are totally dry when they will snap in two, not just bend. Store them in freezer zip bags in your freezer, double-bagged.

To make jalapeño powder, let them defrost and process them to a powder in an electric spice mill. Store the powder in small glass jars with a minimum of head space to reduce oxidation of the powder.

Smoking

After your jalapeños have dried so they've lost about half their weight—a point where they bend, not snap—transfer them to a smoker and treat them with eight hours of smoke. They then will be chipotles. Preferred woods are pecan, oak, and fruit trees. Never use soft wood like pine or fir.

Freezing

Fresh from the garden, wash the pods and cut them lengthwise. Remove the seeds and stems. Double-bag them in freezer zip bags, and squeeze as much air out of the bags as you can. To make them last longer than two or three months in the freezer, turn them into jalapeño mash. After removing the seeds and stems, place them in a food processor or powerful blender and grind them up with a little water until they are a very thick puree. Freeze the mash in plastic containers. Make sure you label and date everything you put in the freezer.

Sun-Cured Pickled Jalapeños

These pickled chiles have an East Indian flavor because of the mustard seeds and ginger. Any small green chiles can be substituted for the jalapeños. Serving suggestion: Serve these unusual chiles on sandwiches, hamburgers, or as a side relish for grilled or roasted meats. Note: This recipe requires advance preparation.

> 1 cup jalapeño chiles, stems and seeds removed, cut in 1/4-inch strips
> 1 tablespoon coarse salt
> 1 tablespoon mustard seeds
> 1 teaspoon cumin seeds
> 1/4 cup oil, peanut preferred
> 1 teaspoon chopped fresh ginger
> 1/4 cup freshly squeezed lemon juice

Sprinkle the chile strips with the salt; toss and let them sit for ten minutes.

Toast the mustard and cumin seeds on a hot skillet for a couple of minutes, stirring constantly, until the seeds begin to crackle and "pop."

Heat the oil to 350 degrees, remove from the heat, stir in the ginger, and let simmer for two minutes. Remove the ginger and discard.

Stir in the chiles, cumin seeds, and lemon juice, and pack in a sterilized jar.

For five days, set the jar in the sun in the morning on days when it is at least seventy degrees, and bring it in at night. Shake the jar a couple of times each day.

Yield: 1 pint   **Heat scale:** Hot

JALAPEÑO JELLY

This goes well on crackers with cream cheese or as a basting sauce for grilled poultry.

- 8 jalapeño chiles, stems and seeds removed
- 2 medium green bell peppers, stems and seeds removed
- 1¼ cup white vinegar
- 1/4 cup lemon juice
- 5 cups sugar
- 6 ounces liquid pectin
- Green food coloring as needed

Place the jalapeños and bell peppers in a blender or processor and chop, being careful not to grind the peppers too finely.

Combine the vinegar, lemon juice, and sugar in a large kettle and bring to a rolling boil. Add the chiles, along with any juice, and boil rapidly for ten minutes, stirring occasionally and removing any foam that forms. Add the pectin and food coloring. Bring back to a boil for an additional minute while stirring constantly.

Skim off any foam that forms, and bottle in clean, sterilized jars.

Yield: 5 cups **Heat scale:** Hot

Salsas, Sauces, and Dressings

Salsa de Jalapeño Asado (Roasted Jalapeño Salsa)

The simplicity of this salsa, imported from northern Mexico and popular in Texas, is deceiving, for it is one of the best all-around table sauces. The charred tomatoes and chiles have a robust flavor, and you can control the texture.

> 2 large tomatoes
> 2 jalapeño chiles, stems removed
> 1/4 teaspoon salt, or to taste

Grill the tomatoes and chiles by placing them three to six inches above the flames. Turn them often; they should be soft, and the skins should be charred.

In a blender, pulse the tomatoes and chiles for fifteen seconds to the desired consistency. Add salt to taste. The texture is smooth, and the sauce is flecked with tiny bits of the charred chile and tomato skins, which add an interesting flavor.

Yield: 2 to 4 servings **Heat scale:** Medium

Pico de Gallo Salsa

This universal salsa, also known as *salsa fria, salsa cruda, salsa fresca, salsa Mexicana,* and *salsa picante,* is served all over the Southwest and often shows up with nontraditional ingredients such as canned tomatoes, bell peppers, or spices like oregano. Here is the most authentic version. Remember that everything in it should be as fresh as possible, and the vegetables must be hand-chopped. Never, never use a blender or food processor. Pico de gallo is best when the tomatoes come from the garden, not from the supermarket. It can be used as a dip for chips or for spicing up fajitas and other Southwestern specialties. Note: It requires advance preparation, and will keep for only a day or two in the refrigerator.

- 4 jalapeño chiles, seeds and stems removed, chopped fine (or more for a hotter salsa)
- 2 large, ripe tomatoes, finely chopped
- 1 medium onion, chopped fine
- 1/4 cup minced fresh cilantro
- 2 tablespoons vinegar
- 2 tablespoons vegetable oil

Combine all ingredients in a large bowl, mix well, and let the salsa sit, covered, for at least an hour to blend the flavors.

Yield: 3 cups **Heat scale:** Medium

Roasted Jalapeño and Avocado Salsa

Try this salsa over your morning omelet or with grilled fish or chicken. It can also be made with New Mexican green chile or even habaneros. The garam masala used here is a spice mixture available in Asian markets.

- 6 jumbo jalapeño chiles, roasted over a flame and peeled, stems and seeds removed
- 4 red bell peppers, roasted over a flame and peeled, stems and seeds removed
- 3 avocados, pitted and peeled
- 2 cups chopped cilantro
- 3/4 cup chopped parsley
- 1/4 cup freshly squeezed lime juice, Key lime preferred
- 3 cloves garlic
- 3/4 teaspoon garam masala, or substitute imported curry powder
- Pinch salt
- Pinch sugar

Dice the jalapeños and bell peppers into 1/4-inch pieces.

Combine the remaining ingredients in a food processor and process into a smooth paste. Remove to a bowl and stir in the jalapeños and bell peppers.

Yield: About 3 cups **Heat scale:** Hot

Texas Green Sauce

When you order "green sauce" in Texas, this is what you will be served. It differs from New Mexico's green sauce in that the color is derived from tomatillos rather than green chiles. It can be used as a dipping sauce, with enchiladas, or as a topping for grilled poultry or fish.

- 3 pounds tomatillos
- 1 bunch green onions
- 1 small bunch cilantro
- 1 tablespoon garlic in oil
- 2 teaspoons sugar
- 2 teaspoons lime juice
- 1 tablespoon chicken base dissolved in 2 tablespoons water
- 6 jalapeño chiles, stems removed

Roast the tomatillos in a roasting pan under the broiler until they are brown and squishy. Turn them over with a pair of tongs and repeat the process. Take the roasted tomatillos, including all the liquid from the roasting process, combine them with the remaining ingredients in a food processor, and puree.

Simmer this mixture for ten minutes before serving or incorporating into another recipe.

Yield: 4 cups   **Heat scale:** Medium

LONE STAR BBQ SAUCE

This Texas-style barbecue sauce makes a tasty marinade and finishing sauce for barbecued or grilled meats and poultry.

- 1½ cups ketchup
- 3 tablespoons chili powder
- 1½ tablespoons vegetable oil
- 1 tablespoon Worcestershire sauce
- 1/2 cup sugar
- 1/4 cup lemon juice
- 2 cloves garlic, finely chopped
- 3 medium onions, finely chopped
- 1 cup tomato paste
- 1½ cups Lone Star Beer (or any other lager)
- 3 jalapeño chiles, seeds and stems removed, finely chopped

In a large saucepan, bring all the ingredients to a boil. Reduce the heat and cover the pan. Let the mixture simmer for one hour, stirring occasionally.

Yield: 4 to 5 cups   **Heat scale:** Medium

Cantina Chile con Queso

Chile con Queso can be served as a dip for tostada chips, as a sauce for topping hamburgers, or even as a thick soup.

> 4 jalapeño chiles, stems removed, seeded, and chopped
> 3 medium onions, quartered
> 2 pounds fresh tomatoes, quartered
> 1/4 cup vegetable oil
> 5 pounds sliced American cheese
> 1 pound grated cheddar cheese
> 6 medium eggs, beaten
> 1 tablespoon chicken base

Boil the jalapeños in two quarts of water for five minutes. Add the tomatoes and onions and boil for ten minutes. Drain the vegetables and retain three cups of water. In a blender, blend the vegetables and the retained water on the lowest speed for five to seven seconds.

In a large pan, saute this puree in the oil over medium heat for ninety seconds. Lower the heat and add the American cheese one slice at a time, allowing it to melt slowly, stirring constantly.

Add the cheddar cheese and stir until completely melted. Combine the eggs with the chicken base in a bowl, mix, and add to the cheese. Cook for five minutes, stirring constantly.

Yield: 12 or more servings as a dip   **Heat scale:** Medium

Creamy Jalapeño Dressing

The use of watercress gives this dressing peppery overtones, and the jalapeños are what really give it some zing. It is good served over salad greens, as well as poured over tender-crisp cooked vegetables such as asparagus. You might even like it as a dip for carrots, jicama, turnip spears, and celery.

- 1 small bunch parsley, washed and drained
- 1 bunch watercress, washed and drained
- 1/2 cup canola oil
- 1/2 cup olive oil
- 1 clove garlic
- 1/3 cup tarragon vinegar
- 2 jalapeño chiles, seeds and stems removed
- 2 shallots, cut in fourths
- 2 teaspoons dry mustard
- 1 tablespoon horseradish
- 1 teaspoon soy sauce
- 1/4 cup plain yogurt

Combine all the ingredients in a food processor or blender and puree. If the mixture seems too thick, add a few teaspoons of yogurt or ice water.

Yield: 2 cups   **Heat scale:** Medium

JALAPEÑO AND PIÑON PESTO FOR PASTA

There's nothing like a quick and spicy Southwestern pesto. Substitute basil or Italian parsley for the cilantro to vary the flavor. Cook up a pot of your favorite pasta and toss it in this pesto.

- 1 cup low-fat sour cream
- 1 cup low-fat plain yogurt
- 1/2 cup piñon nuts, minced
- 1 bunch of fresh cilantro
- 1 jalapeño, seeds and stem removed, chopped (or more, to taste)
- 4 cloves of garlic, peeled
- 1 teaspoon lemon juice
- Salt and freshly ground black pepper to taste

In a food processor, puree the sour cream, yogurt, and piñons until the nuts are finely minced. Add the cilantro, jalapeño, garlic, lemon juice, salt, and pepper, and puree until smooth.

Yield: 2 cups **Heat scale:** Mild

Breakfast

TEX-MEX HUEVOS RANCHEROS

Although the recipes may vary from place to place, the bottom line with ranch-style eggs is that they are delicious for a hearty breakfast or a brunch served with refried beans and hash brown potatoes.

> 4 jalapeño chiles, stems and seeds removed, chopped
> 1 small onion, chopped
> 2 tablespoons vegetable oil
> 2 medium tomatoes, chopped
> 4 corn tortillas
> Vegetable oil for frying
> 8 eggs
> 1/2 cup grated Monterey Jack cheese for garnish

Saute the jalapeños and onions in the oil until soft. Add the tomatoes and cook down to a thick sauce.

Heat a couple of inches of oil in a pan. Fry each tortilla in the oil for only a few seconds a side until soft; remove and drain on paper towels.

Fry each egg to desired consistency.

To serve, place the sauce on each tortilla and gently slip the eggs on top of the sauce. Garnish with the grated cheese and serve.

Yield: 4 servings **Heat scale:** Medium

Chorizo and Jalapeño Egg Scramble

This is a quick, easy, spicy, and delicious way to start the day. Serve the eggs with tortillas or corn muffins, hash brown potatoes, and sliced fruits such as bananas, mangos, or avocados. Note that chorizo sausage is usually loose and not stuffed into a casing.

> 1/2 pound uncooked chorizo
> 2 jalapeño chiles, seeds and stems removed, minced
> 6 eggs, well beaten
> 1 cup prepared mild New Mexican red chile sauce, or more to taste
> 2/3 cup grated cheddar or Monterey Jack cheese

In a large skillet, brown the chorizo and jalapeños together until the chorizo is cooked through, and drain the fat from the skillet. Over medium heat, add the eggs and scramble them to the desired consistency in the chorizo mixture. Transfer the mixture to individual plates, spoon the red chile sauce over the chorizo mixture, and top with the cheese.

Yield: 4 servings **Heat scale:** Medium-hot

Appetizers, Soups, and Salads

Jalapeño Cherry Bombs

These little explosions make perfect appetizers for chilehead guests. Jack-in-the-Box bravely sells Stuffed Jalapeños as its nod to America's growing taste for heat. Of the few spicy offerings available in fast food land, this is the hottest. Dipped in bland bread crumbs, stuffed with American cheese, and deep-fat fried, it is still a jalapeño chile, bless Jack's heart. Here's how to make better ones.

> 24 jalapeño chiles
> 8 ounces Monterey Jack or cheddar cheese, sliced
> Flour for dredging
> 2 eggs, beaten
> Vegetable oil for deep-fat frying

Slit each pepper, remove the seeds with a small spoon or knife, and stuff the peppers with pieces of cheese. If necessary, insert a toothpick to hold the chiles together.

Dip each stuffed chile in the flour, then the egg, then the flour again. Fry in 350-degree oil until the chiles are golden brown. Drain and serve.

Variations: Stuff the chiles with cooked chorizo, or cooked ground meat mixed with cheese.

Yield: 24 bombs **Heat scale:** Medium to hot

El Paso Nachos

This appetizer has become so popular that you don't have to travel to Texas to enjoy it, although "nachos" you buy outside the Southwest may bear little resemblance to the real thing.

> 3/4 cup refried pinto or black beans
> 1/2 pound grated sharp cheddar cheese
> 1/2 cup sour cream
> 4 or more jalapeño chiles, stems and seeds removed, sliced in thin rings

In a large skillet, fry the tortillas in 1 1/2 inches of oil, at 350 degrees, until crispy. Remove and drain on paper towels.

Arrange the tortillas on a pan or oven-proof plate. Place a small amount of beans on each chip, and top with the grated cheese. Heat the pan under the broiler until the cheese melts, or microwave the plate for three to four minutes.

Top with the sour cream and jalapeño slices and serve immediately.

Yield: 6 to 8 servings   **Heat scale:** Medium

Armadillo Eggs

Do armadillos, which are mammals, lay eggs like the Australian platypus? Not really. They're a version of jalapeño poppers that are popular at barbecue cookoffs. They seems to have been invented in 1972 as a food dish at an armadillo festival in Victoria, Texas, and were served with dill pickles, of all things. In this incarnation, the "eggs" are baked, but they can also be grilled, smoked, or deep-fried. A variation uses bacon instead of sausage

- 4 ounces cream cheese, at room temperature
- 1/4 cup sharp cheddar cheese, shredded (about 2 ounces)
- 1 clove garlic, minced
- 1 teaspoon chopped cilantro
- 1/4 teaspoon ground cumin
- Salt to taste
- 6 medium-sized jalapeños, stems removed, cut in half lengthwise, seeds removed, then cut into quarters
- 2 pounds breakfast sausage or other spicy uncooked sausage, removed from the casings

Preheat the oven to 375 degrees, and lightly grease a baking sheet.

In a bowl, use a fork to mix together the cream cheese, cheddar cheese, garlic, cilantro, and cumin until well-blended. Add salt to taste if you wish.

Place about a teaspoon of the cream cheese filling in each jalapeño quarter. Take about 1/3 cup of the sausage and pat it into a three-inch circle, and place the stuffed jalapeño in the center of the sausage. Wrap the sausage completely around the stuffed jalapeño and form into the shape of an egg. Continue until all the jalapeño quarters are wrapped.

Place the "eggs" on the baking sheet about an inch apart. Bake for fifteen to twenty minutes, or until the sausage is cooked. For additional browning, place the sheet under the broiler for two minutes.

Serve with the jalapeño dressing, chile con queso, or any salsa in this book.

Yield: 24 armadillo eggs   **Heat scale:** Medium

TEXAS TOOTHPICKS

"Texas toothpicks" is a 1990s name for jalapeño peppers and onions that are shaved into thin straws, dipped in a batter, and deep fried. The term "Texas toothpicks" is used in restaurants and bars across the country, so whether it originated in Texas is unknown. This version is deep fried, but you can also bake them on parchment paper on top of a baking sheet.

> 4 jumbo green or red jalapeño chiles
> 1 large red onion, separated into layers
> 1 cup all-purpose flour
> 1 teaspoon salt
> 1 teaspoon ground black pepper
> 1 teaspoon garlic powder
> 2 eggs
> 1 cup beer
> 2 cups peanut oil
> Salt to taste

Cut the jalapeños in half lengthwise, and remove the stems and seeds. Using a very sharp knife, cut the jalapeño halves into thin strips about 1/16 inch wide. Separate the onion into rings and cut them to the same length as the jalapeño strips. Mix the two sets of "toothpicks" together in a bowl.

Mix the flour, salt, pepper, garlic powder, eggs, and beer together in another bowl to make a batter. Set the deep fryer to 365 degrees, and heat the oil. Dip the "toothpicks" in the batter to cover, add them to the deep fryer, and fry until they are golden brown and crispy. Remove, drain on paper towels, and transfer to a bowl. Lightly salt them and serve.

Yield: 6 servings   **Heat scale:** Medium

Jalapeño Rings with Chorizo Cream Cheese

My friend Lula Bertrán, from Mexico City, credits the invention of this recipe to her husband, Alberto. "He likes onion rings," she said. "One day while eating them, he said, 'Why don't you do this with chiles?'"

> 2 cups water
> 4 large jalapeños, roasted, peeled, seeds and stems removed, cut into rings
> 3 tablespoons vinegar
> 1/2 cup flour
> 1/2 teaspoon baking powder
> 1/2 teaspoon salt
> 1/2 cup milk
> Vegetable oil for deep frying
> 1/2 cup fried chorizo sausage
> 1/2 cup cream cheese

Preheat the oven to 200 degrees.

Heat the water on high in a large saucepan until it boils. Next, add the jalapeño rings and vinegar to the boiling water, and cook for five minutes. Remove from the heat and cool. Drain the rings and pat dry.

Combine the flour, baking powder, salt, and milk in a bowl to make a batter. Dip the rings into the batter and fry in hot oil until they are crisp and brown. Drain on paper towels.

Combine the chorizo with the cheese to make a paste. Fill the rings with the paste, warm in the oven, and serve hot.

Serves: 4 **Heat scale**: Medium

Clams Pica-Pica

I first tried these clams at a small restaurant in Juarez, Mexico, and liked them so much that they were included in my second book with Nancy Gerlach, *Fiery Appetizers!* You may substitute small oysters or mussels for the clams.

> 4 jalapeño chiles, stems and seeds removed, chopped
> 1 large tomato, peeled and chopped
> 1 small onion, minced
> 2 cloves garlic, minced
> 1 tablespoon lime juice
> 12 large clams in the shell
> Garnishes: Chopped fresh cilantro and
>   thinly sliced onions

Place the chiles, tomato, minced onion, garlic, and lime juice in a blender or food processor and puree until smooth.

Open the clams and discard the top shell, leaving the meat in the bottom of the shell. Place the clams in a shallow pan, meat side up. Place a small amount of the sauce on each clam and bake for fifteen minutes.

Serve with the garnishes on a side platter and a frosty Mexican beer.

Yield: 12 bivalves   **Heat scale:** Hot

CARIOCA BLACK BEAN SOUP

Turtle beans, or black beans, have always been a favorite in both Central and South America, and are gaining in popularity in the U.S. All that is needed to complement this hearty soup is some crusty bread and a crisp garden salad.

- 6 jalapeño chiles, stems and seeds removed, chopped
- 1 large onion, chopped
- 2 cloves garlic, minced
- 1 tablespoon vegetable oil
- 1½ cups black beans, soaked overnight, drained
- 1 large ham hock
- 1/2 teaspoon ground cumin
- 6 to 8 cups chicken broth
- 1 1/2 tablespoons red wine vinegar
- 2 tomatoes, peeled and diced
- 2 tablespoons dry sherry
- 1 tablespoon chopped fresh cilantro

Saute the chiles, onion, and garlic in the oil until soft.

Combine the beans, onion mixture, ham hock, cumin, and broth, then bring to a boil, reduce the heat, and simmer until the beans are soft, about an hour and a half. Add the vinegar and tomatoes and simmer for an additional half-hour.

Remove the ham hock, shred the meat, and set aside.

Puree the bean mixture, if desired, until smooth. You can leave the beans whole. Return to the saucepan and stir in the sherry and reheat.

To serve, stir in the shredded ham and top with the cilantro.

Yield: 6 to 8 servings   **Heat scale:** Medium-hot

"Nevada Annie" Harris's 1978 World Championship Chili

This classic recipe won the International Chili Society championship in 1978. In these competitions, the contestants are used to big competitions and cook huge amounts of chile, so exact proportions are not so critical. Home cooks can certainly cut this recipe in half.

- 3 medium onions, diced
- 2 green bell peppers, stems and seeds removed, diced
- 2 large stalks celery, diced
- 2 small cloves garlic, minced
- 3 jalapeño chiles, stems and seeds removed, minced
- 2 tablespoons vegetable oil
- 4 pounds coarsely ground lean chuck
- 1 can diced green chiles (7 ounces)
- 2 bottles commercial chili powder (3 ounces each)
- 2 cans stewed tomatoes (14 ounces each)
- 1 can tomato sauce (15 ounces)
- 1 can tomato paste (6 ounces)
- 2 tablespoons ground cumin
- Hot sauce to taste
- 1 can beer (12 ounces)
- 1 bottle mineral water (12 ounces)
- 2 to 3 bay leaves
- 1/4 teaspoon garlic salt
- Salt and pepper to taste

In a large stock pot, saute the onions, green peppers, celery, garlic, and jalapeños in the oil until soft. Add the beef and continue to cook until the meat is browned.

Add the remaining ingredients, including half can of beer (drink the remainder, Annie says), and just enough water to cover the top. Bring to a boil, reduce the heat, and simmer for three hours, stirring often. Taste and adjust the seasonings.

Yield: 8 to 12 servings   **Heat scale:** Medium

Cold Gazpacho with Red Hot Chile Salsa

This cool soup with a spicy bite is very refreshing on a hot day. Technically not really cooking, it's a great way to "recycle" any leftover salsa. For a creamier gazpacho, add a mashed ripe avocado.

> 1 cup pico de gallo (page 21)
> 1 small cucumber, peeled and diced
> 3 cups tomato juice
> 2 tablespoons red wine, optional
> 1 tablespoon lime juice
> 1 teaspoon Worcestershire sauce
> Salt to taste
> Chopped fresh cilantro for garnish

Place all the ingredients except the cilantro in a blender or food processor and puree until smooth. Refrigerate for a couple of hours until well chilled.

Yield: 4 servings   **Heat scale:** Medium

Salata Mechouia

Some of the best known Tunisian foods are the grilled salads. The vegetables are roasted before they are combined, giving a "cooked" taste to the salad. It is traditionally prepared over a brazier, then pulverized in a mortar and served spread on chunks of French baguettes or as a relish or salsa with fish and meats. Prepare this dish when fresh tomatoes are available, and experiment with combinations of vegetables.

- 2 jalapeño peppers, stems removed
- 1 medium bell pepper (do not peel)
- 4 medium tomatoes (do not peel)
- 4 cloves garlic (do not peel)
- 2 tablespoons olive oil
- 1 tablespoon lemon juice
- 1/4 teaspoon ground cumin
- 1 tablespoon capers (optional)

Grill the peppers, tomatoes, bell pepper, and garlic on a charcoal grill, over an open gas flame, or under the broiler until the skins blacken and crack. Remove, cool, peel, and remove the stems and seeds.

Either coarsely chop or blend the vegetables, depending on the consistency you desire. Add the remaining ingredients and let sit for half an hour at room temperature to blend the flavors.

Serve with bread or chips as a dip, as a relish to accompany grilled fish or poultry, or on shredded lettuce as a salad.

Variation: Add a small can of drained tuna to the salad after chopping and garnish with two hard-cooked egg wedges.

Yield: 2 to 2½ cups   **Heat scale:** Medium

West African Fiery Groundnut Chop (Chicken and Peanut Stew)

> 5 pieces of chicken, such as legs or thighs
> 1 tablespoon ground ginger
> 3 tablespoons peanut oil, or substitute vegetable oil
> 1 medium onion, chopped
> 3 hot jalapeño chiles, stems and seeds removed, chopped fine
> 2 cloves garlic, minced
> 1 teaspoon minced ginger
> 1 tablespoon hot curry powder
> Pinch ground cumin
> 1 cup canned crushed tomatoes
> 3 cups chicken broth
> 1 cup diced yams or potatoes
> 1 cup frozen okra or green beans
> 1 cup smooth peanut butter
> Salt and freshly ground black pepper
> 1/4 cup chopped salted peanuts

Rub the ground ginger over the chicken pieces.

In a heavy casserole, heat the oil over medium heat until hot. Add the chicken and brown, turning frequently so it doesn't burn. Remove and keep warm.

Pour off all but a tablespoon of the oil, add the onions and saute for three to four minutes, scraping the browned pieces from the bottom of the pan. Add the jalapeños, garlic, and ginger, and saute for a couple of minutes until the onions are lightly browned. Add the curry powder and cook, stirring constantly, until fragrant, about two minutes.

Add the tomatoes and 1 cup of the broth. Raise the heat and bring to a boil, scraping any remaining bits and pieces from the bottom of the pot. Reduce the heat, add the remaining broth and chicken pieces, and simmer uncovered for thirty minutes. Add the yams and okra and continue to simmer until the vegetables are just tender and the chicken is done, about twenty to thirty minutes. Add more broth and water if needed.

Mix the peanut butter with 1 cup of cold water to make a smooth paste. Add 1/2 cup of stew liquid to the paste and mix well. Stir this mixture into the stew and continue simmering until the stew is hot and the chicken is done.

Groundnuts are peanuts in Africa, and "chop" refers to dishes with finely chopped meat in them. There are many variations on this dish in various African countries, but this hearty selection has the most ingredients I've seen. Serve it with bread and beer.

Yield: 4 to 6 servings   **Heat scale:** Medium

Main Dishes and Vegetarian Sides

La Junta Jalapeño Steaks

This recipe is from Nancy Gerlach, who, with her husband, Jeff, accompanied my wife, Mary Jane, and myself to Costa Rica. She wrote: "On the way back to San Jose from the habanero fields in Los Chiles, we stopped at the restaurant La Junta to sample some of the local beef. After enjoying an appetizer of black bean puree, flour tortillas, and cilantro salsa, we were served thick, tender steaks topped with a mild jalapeño sauce."

- 1 tablespoon olive oil
- 4 tablespoons butter or margarine
- 4 boneless steaks, cut 1-inch thick
- 1/4 cup minced onions
- 3 jalapeño chiles, seeds and stems removed, minced
- 1/2 cup red wine
- 1 tablespoon coarsely ground black pepper
- 1½ cups beef stock
- 1/3 cup heavy cream
- 3 jalapeño chiles, stems and seeds removed, cut in thin strips
- 2 tablespoons chopped fresh cilantro

Heat the olive oil and 2 tablespoons of butter in a heavy skillet. Brown the steaks on both sides. Reduce the heat and cook gently to the desired doneness. Remove from the pan and keep warm.

Pour off the fat. Add the remaining butter to the remaining

juices. Add the onion and minced jalapeños and simmer, stirring constantly, until softened.

Add the red wine, bring to a boil, and deglaze the pan, being sure to scrape up any bits that may have stuck to the bottom or sides of the pan. Add the ground black pepper, stock, and cream, and bring to a boil. Reduce the heat and simmer until the sauce is smooth and thick.

Place the steaks on a plate, pour the sauce over the top, garnish with the jalapeño slices and cilantro, and serve.

Yield: 4 servings   **Heat scale:** Medium

Xinjiang Lamb and Chile Barbecue

Xinjiang, which borders Mongolia, is noted for its barbecued lamb even though lamb is rarely eaten in other parts of China. In fact, the Mongolian tribes introduced lamb to the rest of China. This simple barbecue could easily be prepared by the nomads on the plains of Xinjiang.

> 1/4 cup peanut oil
> 8 whole jalapeño chiles, cut in half lengthwise, seeds and stems removed
> 1/2 cup fresh lemon juice
> 2 tablespoons rice wine
> 4 cloves garlic, minced
> 2 teaspoons crushed Sichuan peppercorns
> 1/4 teaspoon salt
> 1/4 teaspoon sugar
> 2 pounds lamb, cut in 1-inch cubes
> 6 sesame seed buns
> Chopped scallions, including the greens
> Chopped cilantro

Combine the chile oil, lemon juice, rice wine, garlic, peppercorns, salt, and sugar. Marinate the lamb and jalapeños in the refrigerator overnight or for two to three hours at room temperature.

Thread the lamb on skewers, alternating with the jalapeños.

Barbecue or broil, basting frequently with the reserved marinade until done.

Serve the lamb and chiles in the buns with the chopped scallions and cilantro.

Yield: 6 servings   **Heat scale:** Medium-hot

THAI CRAB-FRIED RICE

Peter Aiken paddled a kayak to the floating markets of Bangkok while on assignment during the early days of *Chile Pepper* magazine. There, he discovered that while white rice in the region is eaten with meals, fried rice is a meal in itself, often made from leftover rice and other ingredients, and is cooked and served with nam prik sauce. It is quite salty, high in vitamins, and takes some getting used to.

- 2 tablespoons peanut oil
- 1 medium onion, minced
- 2 jalapeño chiles, seeds and stems removed, minced
- 2 cloves garlic, minced
- 3 cups cooked white rice
- 1 cup crabmeat
- 2 eggs
- 3 green onions, sliced
- Lime wedges

Heat the oil in a wok, add the onion, chile, and garlic, and stir fry for a minute on high heat. Add the rice and crabmeat, and heat. Push the rice mixture to the side. Add the eggs to the center and, while stirring continuously, cook until the eggs are half done, then stir the rice into the eggs. Add the green onions just before removing from the heat. The cooking is a five-minute process. Squeeze fresh lime over the finished recipe and serve.

Yield: 4 servings **Heat scale:** Medium

Jalapeños Rellenos (Stuffed Jalapeño Chiles)

This recipe is adapted from Na Conce's 1951 book *Creole Cookery: The Art of Cooking Peruvian Food*. Of course, she used the large, round rocoto chiles, the only kind with black seeds, but the huge jalapeños work well. The red ones are sweeter than the green ones. The heat factor in this dish can be very high, but the other ingredients will temper it somewhat. Serve with hot slices of fresh corn and rounds of sweet potatoes, as they would in Peru.

>   20 red jumbo jalapeño chiles
>   Water to cover
>   1 pound pork, cubed
>   3 cups water
>   2 tablespoons vegetable oil
>   2 onions, chopped
>   2 cloves garlic, minced
>   1 cup peanuts, toasted and ground
>   1 pound cooked green peas
>   1/2 teaspoon salt
>   1/4 teaspoon freshly ground black pepper
>   2 hard-boiled eggs, diced
>   4 eggs, separated
>   Vegetable oil for frying

Wash the chiles, leave the stems intact, open halfway, and carefully remove the seeds. Place the peppers in a large pot, cover with water, and boil the chiles slowly for three minutes. Drain carefully, keeping them intact, and set aside.

Place the pork in a medium saucepan, add the 3 cups of water, and bring to a boil. Lower the heat to a simmer and cook for one hour, or until the pork is tender. Drain the mixture and reserve the cooking liquid. Grind the pork using a coarse setting on the grinder, and set aside.

Heat the oil in a medium skillet and saute the onions and garlic. Add the ground pork, peanuts, peas, salt, pepper, and enough of the reserved pork stock to keep the mixture moist. Mix in the chopped eggs, remove from the heat, and let the mixture cool for a few minutes.

Stuff the chiles with this mixture and close them as tightly as possible.

Beat the egg whites until they are quite stiff, then fold the well-beaten egg yolks into the whites.

Heat the oil in a large skillet, and when it is ready, dip each pepper into the egg mixture and deep fry for thirty to sixty seconds, until the outside is golden brown.

Yield: 20 stuffed chiles   **Heat scale:** Hot

Jalapeño-Smoked Chicken Fajita-Style with Grilled Onion Guacamole

Purists insist that fajitas can be made only with beef skirt steak, so let's just say that this dish was inspired by South Texas fajitas.

Grilled Onion Guacamole:
2 tablespoons corn oil
2 tablespoons fresh lemon juice
1 tablespoon red wine vinegar
1 teaspoon crushed black pepper
1 teaspoon ground whole cumin seeds
3/4 teaspoon salt
1 large red onion, sliced 1/4-inch thick
3 ripe avocados, peeled, pitted, and diced
1 large tomato, diced
2 cloves garlic, minced
1 small bunch fresh cilantro, chopped
2 teaspoons fresh lime juice
3 jalapeño chiles, stems removed, seeded, and chopped fine

Chicken Fajita-Style:
3 jalapeño chiles, stems removed, 2 seeded, all minced
1/8 teaspoon ground cayenne
4 boned, skinned chicken breasts
1 large onion, sliced
2 shallots, chopped
1 small bunch cilantro, chopped
1½ teaspoons crushed black pepper
1½ cups dark beer
1/2 cup corn oil
8 warm flour tortillas

To make the Grilled Onion Guacamole, combine the first six ingredients for a marinade and mix well. Add the onion slices, and marinate for one hour. Drain off the marinade, and grill the onion slices on a hot grill for three minutes per side. Mix the slices with the remaining ingredients, including the jalapeños, and keep at room temperature until ready for use.

To make the fajitas, combine the chicken breasts and the other ingredients except the tortillas, and marinate for two hours at room temperature.

Prepare the smoker, remove the breasts from the marinade, and smoke, using as little heat as possible for fifteen to twenty minutes. Return the breasts to the marinade for another hour.

Prepare a grill, making sure the grate is clean and oiled. Remove the chicken from the marinade, and grill on one side for four minutes. Turn and grill the other side for three minutes. When done, cut the breasts into thin strips.

Serve the chicken with flour tortillas, the guacamole, and the pico de gallo. Guests can roll the chicken with the two sauces in the tortillas.

Yield: 4 servings **Heat scale:** Medium

Jalapeño Pasta

Nanette Blanchard developed this method for making hot and spicy pasta. She wrote: "This pasta has a great fresh chile smell and a golden color with green flecks."

> 6 jalapeño chiles, stems and seeds removed, coarsely chopped
> 3 large eggs, at room temperature
> 2 teaspoons olive oil
> 2 cups unbleached flour
> 2 tablespoons water
> Additional water or flour if needed to adjust consistency.

Put the jalapeño, eggs, and oil in a blender or food processor and puree. If using a processor, add the flour and continue processing until the dough forms a ball. If making the dough by hand, mound the flour on a work surface, make an indentation in the middle it to hold the eggs, then add the egg mixture to the middle of the flour. With a fork, slowly incorporate the flour into the middle of the mixture.

If the mixture remains crumbly, add water one teaspoon at a time until the dough forms a ball. Knead by hand for several minutes to increase the dough's elasticity.

Using a pasta machine or a rolling pin and a well-floured work area, roll the dough out as thinly as possible. Let the sheets of rolled dough dry for about ten minutes before cutting.

With a sharp knife or a pasta machine, cut the sheets into thin strips to the desired width and hang overnight to dry.

To cook, gently immerse in boiling salted water for several minutes or until tender. Serve with your favorite pasta sauce topped with authentic Parmesan cheese.

Yield: 3/4 pound   **Heat scale:** Medium

FRIED CHICKEN WITH GREEN CHILE

This Vietnamese chicken dish is half fried and half braised in the coconut milk. Serve with a salad and a *pho* soup.

- 1 tablespoon peanut oil
- 1/2 onion, sliced
- 1 chicken, cut into large pieces
- 2 teaspoons salt
- 2 teaspoons freshly ground black pepper
- 1 tablespoon fish sauce (nam pla)
- 2 cups coconut milk
- 5 shallots, peeled and sliced
- 14 green onions, white part only
- 3 jalapeño chiles, seeds and stems removed, chopped
- Chopped cilantro for garnish

Heat the oil in a wok. Rub the chicken with the salt and pepper. When the oil is hot, put in the sliced onion and chicken. Fry the chicken until it is golden brown, then add the fish sauce and enough coconut milk to cover. Cook over a low heat until the chicken parts are well done.

In a separate pan, saute the shallots and chiles in the oil until they are fragrant. Next, add the green onions. Transfer the chicken to the shallot mixture, and mix well. Arrange the chicken on a platter and garnish with the cilantro.

Yield: 4 servings **Heat scale:** Medium-hot

JALAPEÑO- AND CHEESE-STUFFED BACON-WRAPPED GRILLED BURGERS

This is the height of burger decadence. Since the bacon will add to the fat content, it's best to use lean ground chuck for these burgers. Since I have been grilling burgers for sixty years, no one knows more about them than I do (heh, heh), so believe it when I tell you the only permissible condiment with them is ketchup. Mustard and mayonnaise are *verboten*. These burgers will be large and thick, and should be cooked to the medium side of medium-rare. The cheese will add moisture, so even when medium, the burgers will be juicy. Serve with—what else?—potato chips and dill or sweet pickles.

> 1½ pounds lean ground chuck
> 3 jalapeño chiles, seeds and stems removed, minced
> 1 cup grated sharp cheddar cheese
> Freshly ground black pepper to taste
> 8 strips raw bacon
> 4 thin slices of a large red onion
> 4 large whole wheat buns with sesame seeds, lightly toasted
> Ketchup as needed

Make eight large patties out of the ground chuck. On four of them, sprinkle the minced jalapeños and cover with the grated cheese. Sprinkle with black pepper to taste. Place the other four patties on top of each one of these and fashion into four thick patties. Wrap two bacon slices around each patty, securing them with toothpicks if necessary.

Grill the patties until they are medium rare or medium. Remove the toothpicks if using, place the burgers on the bottom part of the buns, and add ketchup and the onion slices. Add the top part of the bun and serve.

Yield: 4 servings **Heat scale:** Medium

CURRY SATAY

Satays, also knows as sates, are small brochettes or kabobs, traditionally grilled over charcoal on bamboo skewers in Southeast Asia, Indonesia, and Malaysia. You can used commercial curry powder or make your own, and this recipe also works well with chicken. Red curry paste is available in Asian markets. Serve with Yellow Festive Rice (page 59). For a tasty variation, thread fruits such as banana or pineapple pieces between the pork cubes.

2 pounds boneless pork, cut in 3/4-inch cubes

CURRY PASTE MARINADE:
1/2 cup coconut milk
1/4 cup white vinegar
2 tablespoons red curry paste
2 tablespoons curry powder
1 tablespoon sugar
1½ teaspoons green jalapeño powder

Combine all the ingredients for the marinade in a bowl, add the pork, cover, and marinate the pork for two hours at room temperature. Remove the pork and simmer the marinade in a pan for twenty minutes. Thread the pork on the skewers, putting about half a dozen on each. Leave a two- or three-inch "handle" at one end, and pack the meat close together. Grill the skewers for about ten minutes over a medium-hot heat, basting frequently with the marinade, until browned and crisp. Cut open a sample to check for doneness.

Serve the satays accompanied by a commercial Asian chile sauce.

Yield: 4 to 6 servings or 24 skewers **Heat scale:** Medium

Grilled Jalapeño Polenta with Roasted Salsa Verde

Roasted salsas are all the rage, so here's a practical application of the concept. And while we're at it, we'll add chiles to everything and even grill the polenta. Serve as an entree with a vegetable and a salad or as a side to grilled meat or chicken.

Grilled Jalapeño Polenta:
3/4 cup coarse yellow cornmeal
1½ cups milk
1/2 cup grated cheddar or Asiago cheese
2 jalapeño chiles, stems and seeds removed, chopped
2 tablespoons grated onion
1 clove garlic, minced
3 tablespoons olive oil
Salt to taste

Roasted Salsa Verde:
1 pound fresh tomatillos, husks left on
1 small onion, quartered
4 jalapeño chiles
2 tablespoons lime juice, fresh preferred
1 teaspoon sugar
1/4 cup chopped fresh cilantro
Salt to taste

For the polenta, bring the milk and 1½ cups of water to a boil in a large saucepan. Slowly sprinkle the cornmeal into the liquid, stirring constantly. Reduce the heat, and continue to stir until the mixture is thick and starts to pull away from the pan. Quickly add the cheese, chiles, onion, and garlic; salt to taste, stir well, and remove from the heat.

Pour the polenta into a lightly oiled ten-inch cake or pie pan, and cool. Place in refrigerator for three hours to firm.

To make the salsa, place tomatillos, onion, and chiles in a basket on the grill and roast until the vegetables are slightly blackened, shaking the basket often. Remove from the basket and peel, but don't worry about removing all the peels from the chiles. Do remove stems and seeds from them. Place the vegetables, juice, and sugar into a blender or food processor and puree until smooth. Season with salt and stir in the cilantro.

Clean the grill and brush it with oil. Slice the polenta into wedges, brush with the oil, and grill over a medium fire until they begin to brown, about eight to twelve minutes.

Place the wedges on a serving platter, top with the salsa, and serve.

Yield: 4 to 6 servings   **Heat scale:** Medium

MEXICALI RICE

Unlike other versions of Spanish rice, which tend to be bland tomato sauce concoctions, ours is crispy and lively with taste. Serve the rice as an accompaniment for enchiladas or spicy grilled vegetables.

- 3 tablespoons olive oil
- 1 cup uncooked long grain rice
- 1 small onion, chopped
- 1/2 cup celery, diced
- 1/4 cup diced bell pepper
- 1 clove garlic, minced
- 2 large tomatoes, peeled, seeded, and coarsely chopped
- 2 jalapeño chiles, seeds and stems removed, minced
- 2 tablespoons chopped fresh cilantro
- 1 teaspoon fresh lime juice
- 1/2 teaspoon oregano
- 2 cups chicken stock
- 1 cup grated sharp cheddar cheese (optional)

Heat the oil in a skillet, and saute the rice over low heat for four to five minutes, until it is golden. Add the onion, celery, bell pepper, and garlic, and saute for one minute. Then add the remaining ingredients (except the cheese), stir, and bring the mixture to a boil. Cover with a tight-fitting lid, turn the heat down to a simmer, and cook for twenty minutes.

Optional: When the rice is done, spread the grated cheese over the top, and cover until the cheese melts.

Serves: 4 to 6 **Heat scale:** Medium

YELLOW FESTIVE RICE
(NASI KUNYIT)

I thank Devagi Shanmugan, who runs the Thomson Cooking School in Singapore, for this rice recipe which makes a very colorful, fragrant dish that goes well with meat. If you ever get to Singapore, be sure to take some of her classes. Remember to use coconut milk, not canned coconut cream, which is too sweet.

- 4 teaspoons ground coriander
- 2 teaspoons ground cumin
- 1 teaspoon ground turmeric
- 1 teaspoon green jalapeño powder
- 1 piece fresh ginger (5 inches), peeled
- 3 cloves garlic, peeled
- 20 shallots, peeled
- 1 cup water
- 6 tablespoons vegetable oil
- 6 cups canned coconut milk
- 3 cups rice, washed and drained
- 4 bulbs lemongrass
- Salt to taste
- Garnish: Fried green onion rings

Puree the first eight ingredients in a blender or food processor. In a heavy skillet, heat the oil, and when it is almost sizzling, add the pureed ingredients and stir until they are fragrant, about one minute.

Add the coconut milk and bring to a slow boil. Reduce the heat to a simmer, add the rice and lemongrass, cover, and cook on low heat until the rice is done—about forty minutes.

Add the salt to taste, and garnish with the fried green onion rings.
Yield: 6 servings **Heat scale:** Medium

Corn, Squash, and Chile Saute (Calabacitas)

This recipe combines two Native American crops, squash and corn, with chile. One of the most popular dishes in New Mexico, it is also so colorful that it goes well with a variety of foods.

- 3 zucchini squash, cubed
- 1/2 cup chopped onion
- 2 cloves garlic minced
- 3 tablespoons vegetable oil
- 1/4 cup chopped jalapeños
- 2 cups whole kernel corn cut from the cob
- 1/2 teaspoon dried oregano
- 1/2 cup cream or half and half
- 1 cup grated Monterey Jack cheese

Saute the squash, onion, and garlic in the oil until the squash is tender. Add the chile, corn, oregano, and cheese, and simmer for ten minutes.

Yield: 4 servings **Heat scale:** Medium

Breads

Jalapeño Focaccia Bread

Jalapeños are the perfect addition to this wonderful Italian bread. Perfect for an hors d'oeuvre or with the meal, this recipe is easily doubled or tripled.

> 2 cups warm tap water (about 110 degrees)
> 2 envelopes active dry yeast
> 12 tablespoons olive oil
> 10 cups unbleached all-purpose flour
> 4 teaspoons salt
> 1/3 cup minced jalapeños that have been sauteed in
>   vegetable oil until soft
> 2 cups milk
> 2 teaspoons coarse salt

Place the water in a bowl, then whisk in the yeast and half the olive oil. In a separate mixing bowl, combine the flour, salt, and jalapeño. Stir the yeast mixture and milk into the flour mixture with a sturdy spatula until the flour is well combined, mixing once vigorously. Cover the bowl with plastic wrap and let the dough rise until it has doubled in size, about one hour.

Spread $1^1/_2$ teaspoons of the oil in two 11x17-inch pans. Turn the dough out of the bowl, and divide between the two pans. Pat and press the dough to fill each pan completely.

If there seems to be too much dough, let it rest and continue in a few minutes. Using your pinky finger, poke cavities in the focaccia about every two inches. Drizzle each pan with equal amounts of the remaining oil, and sprinkle with the coarse salt.

Let the dough rise again until it doubles in size.

Preheat the oven to 450 degrees. Bake the bread on a rack over the lower third of the oven for twenty-five minutes, or until it is a light golden-brown color. Remove from the oven and serve immediately, or cool the pan on a rack for later use. Reheat the bread at 375 degrees for six or seven minutes.

Yield: 2 loaves   **Heat scale:** Medium

BLUE CORN JALAPEÑO MUFFINS

Blue corn, or Indian corn, has become increasingly popular, and there are now blue corn tortillas, corn meal, and chips. It has a nuttier flavor than regular corn and gives these muffins a delightful—and some say shocking—color.

- 1/4 cup minced jalapeño chile
- 1½ cups fine-ground blue cornmeal (available by mail order and from gourmet shops)
- 1 cup all-purpose flour
- 1 tablespoon salt
- 1 tablespoon baking powder
- 2 tablespoons sugar
- 1¾ sticks margarine, melted
- 1/4 cup onions, minced
- 1 clove garlic, minced
- 2 large eggs
- 1 cup milk
- 2 tablespoons fresh cilantro, chopped

Preheat the oven to 450 degrees. Saute the jalapeño in a frying pan with a little vegetable oil until soft, about four minutes. Remove and drain on paper towels.

Combine the cornmeal, flour, salt, baking powder, and sugar in a large bowl. In another bowl, whisk together the margarine, onion, and garlic. Add the eggs, milk, jalapeño, and cilantro, whisking continually.

Add the flour mixture in small amounts until the batter is completely combined. Pour the batter into twelve well-greased half-cup muffin tins. Bake the muffins for eighteen to twenty minutes, or until they are golden. Turn the muffins out onto racks and let them cool.

Yield: 12 muffins **Heat scale:** Medium

A Drink and a Dessert

"Red Ass" Bloody Mary Mix

So named because of his chili team, Mitch "Red Ass Chili" Moody of Long Beach, California, explained the origin of this drink mix which appeared in *Chile Pepper* magazine: "A lot of chili cookoffs start this way, or at least ours do! This mix will spice up your morning, and possibly help with that hangover from the night before. I got the idea from a friend who told me about sangrita, a chaser that is served with tequila shots. Delete the habanero unless you like it extremely hot! I've heard that the mix is also good without alcohol, but I've never tried it that way."

- 1 jalapeño chile, stem and seeds removed
- 1 habanero chile, stem and seeds removed
- 6 tablespoons Worcestershire sauce
- 1/4 cup A-1 sauce
- 2 tablespoons chopped fresh cilantro
- 1 tablespoon horseradish
- 1 tablespoon garlic salt
- 1 teaspoon freshly ground black pepper
- 1/4 teaspoon dried oregano
- Juice of 1/2 lemon
- 1 cup orange juice
- 1 quart tomato juice
- Vodka or tequila
- Salt and mild chile powder
- Lemon or lime slices for garnish

Put the chiles, Worcestershire and A-1 sauces, cilantro, horseradish, garlic salt, pepper, and oregano in a blender and process until smooth. Stir in the juices and chill.

To serve, place the salt and chile powder on a plate. Wet the rim of the serving glasses with a lime slice, and rub the glass upside down on the chile mixture. Pour $1\frac{1}{2}$ ounces of liquor in each glass along with ice, fill with the bloody mary mix, stir well, garnish with a lime slice and serve.

Yield: 1 quart   **Heat scale:** Hot

Mango-Habanero Sorbet

I've added just a hint of jalapeño to give this sorbet a sweet heat punch. Of course, non-chileheads can eliminate it for a purist's dessert. To make a refreshing drink with this sorbet, combine two tablespoons of it with one teaspoon of triple sec over ice, and top with sparkling water. Stir well.

> 3/4 cup water
> 6 tablespoons sugar
> 3 cups freshly squeezed orange juice
> 1/2 jalapeño chile, seeds and stems removed, minced
> 3 tablespoons orange liqueur such as triple sec

In a saucepan, bring the water and the sugar to a boil, stirring well to dissolve the sugar. Pour into a nine-inch cake pan and let cool. Stir in the orange juice and the jalapeño, and cover. Place in the freezer and freeze solid (about two hours).

Break into chunks and beat with an electric mixer or blender until it's slushy. Use immediately or process in an ice cream freezer.

Yield: 6 servings   **Heat scale:** Medium

PART 3
Resources

Further Reading

- DeWitt, Dave and Paul W. Bosland. *The Complete Chile Pepper Book: Choosing, Growing, Preserving, and Cooking.* Portland, OR: Timber Press, 2009.
- DeWitt, Dave. *1001 Best Hot & Spicy Recipes.* Chicago: Surrey Books, 2010.
- DeWitt, Dave. *The Southwest Table: Traditional Foods from Texas, New Mexico, and Arizona.* New York: Lyons Press, 2011.
- DeWitt, Dave. *Dave DeWitt's Chile Trivia.* Albuquerque: Sunbelt Media, 2012.

Seed and Plant Sources

For seeds, go to the Chile Pepper Institute, **www.chilepepperinstitute.org**, Paul W. Bosland, publisher; Danise Coon, editor.

For 500 varieties of chile pepper bedding plants in season and fresh chile pods in the late summer and early fall, go to Cross Country Nurseries, **www.chileplants.com**, Janie Lamson, publisher.

Websites

For detailed information on chile peppers around the world:

- The Fiery Foods and Barbecue SuperSite, **www.fieryfoods.com**, Dave DeWitt, publisher; Lois Manno, editor. This site has more than four hundred articles on chile varieties, gardening, history, cooking, and Q&As.
- The Chile Pepper Institute, **www.chilepepperinstitute.org**, Paul W. Bosland, publisher and director; Danise Coon, editor and assistant director. The shop at this site contains books, chile information, and the seeds for dozens of chile varieties.
- Pepperworld.com, **www.pepperworld.com** (German language), Harald Zoschke, publisher and editor. The site's many articles include European chile-growing information.

- The Chileman, **www.thechileman.org**, Mark McMillan, publisher and editor. This U.K. site contains the best glossary of chile pepper varieties, with about four thousand listed.
- Fatalii.net, **www.fatalii.net**, a Finnish site, in English, with extensive information about chile growing and bonsai chiles. Jukka Kilpinnen is the publisher and editor.
- The Burn! Blog, **www.burn-blog.com**, which keeps chileheads and BBQ freaks in touch with the latest news, personalities, and weirdness in the worlds of chile peppers, spiced-up foods, and barbecues

CHILE PEPPER SUPPLIERS AND ONLINE HOTSHOPS

MexGrocer, **www.MexGrocer.com**, has many varieties of worldwide chiles as dried pods and powders.

Melissa's/World Variety Produce, Inc., **www.melissas.com**, has worldwide fresh chiles in season, as well as a fine collection of dried pods and powders.

Peppers, **www.peppers.com**, has the best selection of chile pepper and barbecue products such as hot sauces, salsas, jams, cookies, candies, rubs, chili mixes—the list is very long.

About the Author

If Dave DeWitt's life were a menu, it would feature dishes as diverse as alligator stew and apple pie à la mode—not to mention the beloved chile peppers that have become the basic ingredient of so many of his projects and accomplishments.

Since starting out in the electronic media, Dave has built careers as a businessman, educator, administrator, producer, on-camera personality, author, and publisher. Currently, in addition to serving as CEO of Sunbelt Shows and co-producer of the National Fiery Foods & Barbecue Show, Dave is always busy sharing his chile pepper expertise in as wide a range of forums as possible.

Besides writing more than forty books (mostly on fiery foods but also including novels, food histories, and travel guides), Dave is publisher of the Fiery Foods & BBQ Super Site (at **www.fieryfoods.com**), and was a founder of Chile Pepper magazine and Fiery Foods & Barbecue magazine.

From his beginning as a radio announcer, Dave went on to own audio/video production companies for which he wrote, produced, and voiced hundreds of radio and television commercials. After moving to New Mexico in 1974, he wrote and hosted the "Captain Space" TV show which beat out both "Saturday Night Live" and "Star Trek" in its Saturday midnight time slot, and, in an entirely different sphere, curated the Albuquerque Museum's 1984 exhibit *Edward S. Curtis in New Mexico*.

The interest in chile peppers and spicy foods that has helped make Dave one of the foremost authorities in the world has led to such best-sellers as *The Whole Chile Pepper Book, The Pepper Garden, The Hot Sauce Bible, The Chile Pepper Encyclopedia,* and *The Spicy Food Lover's Bible*. His latest book on the subject is *Chile Trivia*. As the ultimate testament to his fame and achievement, *The New York Times* has declared him to be "the Pope of Peppers."

Dave is an associate professor in Consumer and Environmental Sciences on the adjunct faculty of New Mexico State University, and also serves as chair of the Board of Regents of the New Mexico Farm and Ranch Heritage Museum.

Made in the USA
Charleston, SC
23 February 2013